S...
of
Blessing

Helen
Steiner Rice

**CHRISTIAN ART
PUBLISHERS**

Seasons of blessing is excerpts of *A Book of Blessings* first published by Fleming H. Revell, a division of Baker Book House Company, P O Box 6287, Grand Rapids, MI 49516-6287

© 1995 by Virginia J. Ruehlmann and
The Helen Steiner Rice Foundation
Compiled by Virginia J. Ruehlmann

Published in South Africa by Christian Art Publishers
P O Box 1599, Vereeniging, 1930

© 1996
First edition 1998

Cover designed by Christian Art Publishers

Scripture quotations marked RSV are taken from the Revised Standard Version of the Bible, copyright 1946, 1952, 1971 and 1973 by the Division of Christian Education of the National Council of the Churches of Christ in the United States of America.

Scripture verses marked NIV are taken from the HOLY BIBLE, NEW INTERNATIONAL VERSION ®. NIV®. Copyright © 1973, 1978, 1984, by International Bible Society. Used by permission of Zondervan Publishing House. All rights reserved.

Scripture selections from the New American Bible (NAB) Copyright © 1970 by the Confraternity of Christian Doctrine, Washington, D.C., are used with permission. All rights reserved.

Printed and bound by Hablo Company Limited, Hong Kong

ISBN 1-86852-231-8

98 99 00 01 02 03 04 05 06 07 – 10 9 8 7 6 5 4 3 2 1

Lovingly I dedicate
each thought herein expressed
To all who read this little book,
and may their lives be blessed ...

Contents

The Helen Steiner Rice Foundation

❧ ❦

Whatever the celebration, whatever the day, whatever the event, whatever the occasion, Helen Steiner Rice possessed the ability to express the appropriate feeling for that particular moment in time.

A happening became happier, a sentiment more sentimental, al memory more memorable because of her deep sensitivity to put into understandable language the emotion being experienced. Her positive attitude, her concern for others, and her love of God are identifiable threads woven into her life, her wordk ... and even her death.

Prior to Mrs. Rice's passing, she established the *Helen Steiner Rice Foundation*, a nonprofit corporation whose purpose is to award grants to worthy charitable programs that assist the elderly and the needy.

Royalties form the sale of this book will add to the financial capabilities of the *Helen Steiner Rice Foundation*. Because of limited resources, the foundation presently limits grants to qualified charitable programs in Lorain,

Ohio, where Helen Steiner Rice was born, and Greater Cincinnati, Ohio, where Mrs. Rice lived and worked most of her life. Hopefully, in the near future, resources will be of sufficient size that broader areas can be considered for the awarding of grants.

Because of her foresight, caring, and deep conviction of sharing, Helen Steiner Rice continues to touch a countless number of lives through grants and through her inspirational poetry.

Virginia J. Reuhlmann, Administrator
The Helen Steiner Rice Foundation
Suite 2100, Atrium Two
221 E. Fourth Street
Cincinatti, Ohio 45201

Introduction

❧   ❦

Wishing God's sweet blessings
Not in droplets but a shower,
To fall on you throughout the day
And brighten every hour.

A pilgrimage to the Holy Land increases one's faith, inspirations, and amazement. Visiting Capernaum and the Sea of Galilee sparks an incredible realization that the visitor is perhaps walking the same path that Jesus traveled when He delivered the Sermon on the Mount. His words in that sermon startled the crowd and challenged the basic attitudes and values of that day – and the present!

Envision Jesus climbing the mountainside with the crowd following, finding a level spot, and sitting down to teach, as was the custom then for rabbis. The listeners were amazed at His message.

The Beatitudes promised that many blessings are available when we live our individual lives in a fashion that is pleasing to God and when we concentrate on important Christian values rather than unimportant worldly aspects.

If Jesus were to deliver His Sermon on the Mount today, our secular world would again be startled. The lessons in the Beatitudes are equally important and timely in the here and now as in the day when spoken originally by Jesus. His priciples stressed a lifestyle of agape love, charity, forgiveness, humility, trust and a dependence upon God rather than the worldly goals of wealth, pleasure, and self-justification.

Helen Steiner Rice endeavored to live by the philosophy espoused by Jesus. Her poetry vividly, effectively, and inspirationally expresses the same spiritual concepts and values that are inherent in the message of the Beatitudes.

May *A Book of Blessings* be a blessing in your life and, by your example and actions, may your life be a blessing to others. Permit God's love to flow through you.

May God's choicest blessings be yours.

– *Virginia J. Reuhlmann* –

BLESSINGS WITHOUT END

*Blessed are the
poor in spirit,
for theirs is the
kingdom of heaven.*

❧ Matthew 5:3 NIV ❧

Put your problems in God's hands

❧ ⚘ ❧

Although it sometimes seems to us
   our prayers have not been heard,
God always knows our every need
   without a single word,
And He will not forsake us
   even though the way is steep,
For He is always near to us,
   a tender watch to keep ...
And in good time He'll answer us,
   and in His love He'll send
Greater things than we have asked
   and blessings without end.
So though we do not understand
   why trouble comes to man,
Can we not be contented
   just to know it is God's plan!

Blessed are all who take refuge in him.

❧ Psalm 2:12 RSV ⚘

❧ 12

A child's prayer

Hear me, blessed Jesus,
  as I say my prayers today.
Tell me You are close to me
  and You'll never go away.
Tell me that You love me
  like the Bible says You do,
And tell me also, Jesus,
  I can always come to You,
And You will understand me
  when other people don't,
And though some may forget me,
  just tell me that You won't ...
And someday when I'm older,
  I will show You it is true
That even as a little child
  my heart belongs to You.

And he took the children in his arms,
put his hands on them and blessed them.

Mark 10:16 NIV

Blessings
in disguise

❧   ❧

God sends His little angels
    in many forms and guises.
They come as lovely miracles
    that God alone devises,
For He does nothing without purpose –
    everything's a perfect plan
To fulfill in bounteous measure
    all He ever promised and ...
Every little angel
    with a body bent and broken
Or a little mind unknowing
    or little words unspoken
Is just God's way of trying
    to reach out and touch the hands
Of all who do not know Him
    and cannot understand
That often through an angel
    whose wings will never fly
The Lord is pointing out
    the way to His eternal sky,
Where there will be no handicaps
    of body, soul, or mind,
And where all limitations

will be dropped and left behind ...
So accept these little angels
    as gifts from God above,
And thank Him for this lesson
    in faith and hope and love.

You shall serve the Lord your God,
and I will bless your bread and
your water; and I will take sickness
away from the midst of you.

❧ Exodus 23:25 RSV ❧

God keep you
in His care

There are many things in life
we cannot understand,
But we must trust God's judgment
and be guided by His hand ...

And all who have God's blessing
can rest safely in His care,
For He promises safe passage
on the wings of faith and prayer.

*O save thy people, and bless thy
heritage: be thou their shepherd,
and carry them for ever.*

Psalm 28:9 RSV

God's sweetest appointments

જી ઉ

Out of life's misery born of man's sins,
A fuller, richer life begins,
For when we are helpless with no place to go
And our hearts are heavy and our spirits are low,
If we place our lives in God's hands
And surrender completely to His will and demands,
The darkness lifts and the sun shines through,
And by His touch we are born anew.
So praise God for trouble that cuts like a knife
And disappointments that shatter your life,
For with patience to wait and faith to endure,
Your life will be blessed and your future secure,
for God is but testing your faith and your love
Before He appoints you to rise far above
All the small things that so sorely distress you,
For God's only intention is to strengthen and
bless you.

Blessed are those who have
learned to acclaim you, who walk in
the light of your presence, O Lord.

જી Psalm 89:15 NIV ઉ

Live by faith and not by feelings

When everything is pleasant and bright
And the things we do turn out just right,
We feel without question that God is real,
For when we are happy, how good we feel,
But when the tides turn and gone is the song
And misfortune comes and our plans go wrong,
Doubt creeps in and we start to wonder
And our thoughts about God are torn
asunder –
For we feel deserted in times of deep stress
Without God's presence to assure us and bless,
And it is when our senses are reeling
We realize clearly it's faith and not feeling,
For it takes great faith to patiently wait,
Believing God comes not too soon or too late.

A faithful man will be richly blessed.

Psalm 28:20 NIV

BLESSINGS FOR ALL SEASONS

*Blessed are those who hunger
and thirst for righteousness,
for they will be filled.*

❧ Matthew 5:6 NIV ❧

How to find happiness

Happiness is something you create in your mind,
Not something you search for but can't seem to find,
Not something that's purchased with silver or gold,
Not something that force can capture and hold.
It's just waking up and beginning each day
By counting your blessings and kneeling to pray.
It's giving up thoughts that breed discontent
And accepting what comes as a gift heavensent.
It's giving up wishing for things you have not
And making the best of whatever you've got.
It's knowing that life is determined and planned
And God holds the world in the palm of His hand.
And it's by completing what God gives you to do
That you find contentment and happiness, too.

*Blessed are they whose ways are
blameless, who walk according
to the law of the Lord.*

Psalm 119:1 NIV

My birthday
in the hospital

How little we know what God has in store
As daily He blesses our lives more and more.
I've lived many years and I've learned many
things,
But today I have grown new spiritual wings ...
For pain has a way of broadening our view
And bringing us closer in sympathy, too,
To those who are living in constant pain
And trying somehow to bravely sustain
The faith and endurance to keep on trying
When they almost welcome the peace of
dying ...
Without this experience I would have lived
and died
Without fathoming the pain of Christ crucified,
For none of us knows what pain is all about
Until our spiritual wings start to sprout.
So thank You, God, for the gift You sent
To teach me that pain's heaven-sent.

Blessed is he who has regard for the weak;
the Lord delivers him in times of trouble.

Psalm 41:1 NIV

Daily prayers
dissolve your cares

❧ ❧

I meet God in the morning
 and go with Him through the day,
Then in the stillness of the night
 before sleep comes I pray
That God will just take over
 all the problems I couldn't solve,
And in the peacefulness of sleep
 my cares will all dissolve.
So when I open up my eyes
 to greet another day,
I'll find myself renewed in strength
 and there will open up a way
To meet what seemed impossible
 for me to solve alone,
And once again I'll be assured
 I am never on my own.
For if we try to stand alone,
 we are weak and we will fall,
For God is always greatest
 when we're helpless, lost, and small.
And no day is unmeetable
 if, on rising, our first thought
Is to thank God for the blessings

that His loving care has brought ...
For there can be no failure
    or hopeless, unsaved sinners
If we enlist the help of God,
    who makes all losers winners.

So meet Him in the morning
    and go with Him through the day,
And thank Him for His guidance
    each evening when you pray –
And if you follow faithfully
    this daily way to pray,
You will never in your lifetime
    face another hopeless day.

> *You also must help us by prayer, so
> that many will give thanks on our
> behalf for the blessing granted
> us in answer to many prayers.*

> ❧ 2 Corinthians 1:11 RSV ❧

Learn to rest

We all need short vacations
in life's fast and maddening race –
An interlude of quietness
from the constant, jet-age pace.
So when your day is pressure-packed
and your hours are all too few,
Just close your eyes and meditate
and let God talk to you ...
For when we keep on pushing,
we're not following in God's way –
We are foolish, selfish robots
mechanized to fill each day
With unimportant trivia
that makes life more complex
And gives us greater problems
to irritate and vex
So when your nervous network
becomes a tangled mess,
Just close your eyes in silent prayer
and ask the Lord to bless
Each thought that you are thinking,
each decision you must make,
As well as every word you speak
and every step you take –
For only by the grace of God

can you gain self-control,
And only meditative thoughts
    can restore your peace of soul.

*But blest are your eyes
because they see and blest are
your ears because they hear.*

❧ Matthew 13:16 NAB ❧

The seasons
of the soul

Why am I cast down and despondently sad
When I long to be happy and joyous and glad!
Why is my heart heavy with unbearable weight
As I try to escape this soul-saddened state!
I ask myself often what makes life this way –
Why is the song silenced in my heart today!
And then with God's help it all becomes clear –

The soul has its seasons just the same as the
year.
I too must pass through life's autumn of dying,
A desolate period of heart-hurt and crying,
Followed by winter, in whose frostbitten hand
My heart is as frozen as the snow-covered land.
We too must pass through the seasons God
sends,
Content in the knowledge that everything
ends.

Praise the Lord. Blessed is the man
who fears the Lord, who finds
great delight in his commands.

Psalm 112:1 NIV

BE GLAD FOR GOD'S BLESSINGS

*Blessed are the pure in
heart, for they will see God.*

❧ Matthew 5:8 NIV ❦

What is a blessing?

The good, green earth beneath your feet,
The air you breathe, the food you eat,
Some work to do, a goal to win,
A sense of peace deep down within –
In these simple things may you always find
Joys of the very greatest kind.

*Bless the Lord, O my soul; and all
that is within me, bless his holy name!*

&ppp; Psalm 103:1 RSV &ppp;

Man cannot live by bread alone

৯১   ৯৫

He lived in a palace on a mountain of gold,
Surrounded by riches and wealth untold,
Priceless possessions and treasures of art,
But he died alone of a hungry heart,
For man cannot live by bread alone
No matter what he may have or own,
For though he reaches his earthly goal,
He'll waste away with a starving soul
But he who eats of the holy bread
Will always find his spirit fed,
And even the poorest of men can afford
To feast at the table prepared by the Lord.

*Do, then, bless the house of your servant
that it may be before you forever; for
you, Lord God, have promised, and
by your blessing the house of your
servant shall be blessed forever.*

৯১ 2 Samuel 7:29 NAB ৯৫

Be glad

Be glad that your life has been full and com-
plete,
Be glad that you've tasted the bitter and sweet.
Be glad that you've walked in sunshine and
rain,
Be glad that you've felt both pleasure and pain.
Be glad that you've had such a full, happy life,
Be glad for your joy as well as your strife.
Be glad that you've walked with courage each
day,
Be glad you've had strength each step of the
way.
Be glad for the comfort that you've found in
prayer,
Be glad for God's blessings, His love, and His
care.

Enter his gates with thanksgiving,
and his courts with praise! Give
thanks to him, bless his name!

❧ Psalm 100:4 RSV ☙

Meet life's
trials with smiles

❧   ❧

There are times when life overwhelms us
   and our trials seem too many to bear –
It is then we should stop to remember
   God is standing by ready to share
The uncertain hours that confront us
   and fill us with fear and despair,
For God in His goodness has promised
   that the cross that He gives us to wear
Will never exceed our endurance
   or be more than our strength can bear.
And secure in that blessed assurance,
   we can smile as we face tomorrow,
For God holds the key to the future,
   and no sorrow or care we need borrow.

*Blessed be the God and Father
of our Lord Jesus Christ, who has
blessed us in Christ with every spiritual
blessing in the heavenly places.*

❧ Ephesians 1:3 NAB ❧

God,
give us drive

❧   ❧

There's a difference between drive and driven –
The one is selfish, the other God-given,
For the driven man has but one goal –
Just wordly wealth and not riches of soul ...
And daily he's spurred on to reach and attain
A higher position, more profit and gain.
Ambition and wealth become his great needs
As daily he's driven by avarice and greed.

But most blessed are they who use their drive
To work with zeal so all men may survive,
For while they forfeit great personal gain,
Their work and their zeal are never in vain,
For they contribute to the whole human race,
And we cannot survive without growing in
grace.

So help us, dear God, to choose between
The driving forces that rule our routine
So we may make our purpose and goal
Not power and wealth but the growth of our
souls,
And give us strength and drive and desire

To raise our standards and ethics higher,
So all of us and not just a few
May live on earth as You want us to.

*Him who monopolizes grain, the
people curse – but blessings upon
the head of him who distributes it!*

ª Proverbs 11:26 NAB ª

BLESSINGS AMID TROUBLE

*Blessed are those who
are persecuted because of
righteousness, for theirs is
the kingdom of heaven.*

☙ Matthew 5:10 NIV ❧

God's assurance gives us endurance

❧   ❧

My blessings are so many,
   my troubles are so few –
How can I be discouraged
   when I know that I have You?
And I have the sweet assurance
   that there's nothing I need fear
If I but keep remembering
   I am Yours and You are near,
Help me to endure the storms
   that keep raging deep inside me,
And make me more aware each day
   that no evil can betide me.
If I remain undaunted
   though the billows sweep and roll,
Knowing I have Your assurance,
   there's a haven for my soul,
For anything and everything
   can somehow be endured
If Your presence is beside me
   and lovingly assured.

Bless the Lord, O my soul
and forget not all his benefits.

❧ Psalm 103:2 RSV ❧

Adversity can bless us

❧   ❧

The way we use adversity
    is strictly our own choice,
For in God's hands
    adversity can make the heart rejoice.
For everything God sends to us,
    no matter in what forml,
Is sent with plan and purpose,
    for by the fierceness of a storm
The atmosphere is changed and cleared
    and the earth is washed and clean,
And the high winds of adversity
    can make restless souls serene.
And while it's very difficult
    for mankind to understand
God's intentions and His purpose
    and the workings of His hand,
If we observe the miracles
    that happen every day,
We cannot help but be convinced
    that in His wondrous way
God makes what seemed unbearable
    and painful and distressing
Easily acceptable

when we view it as a blessing.

The Lord will open to you his good
treasury the heavens, to give the rain
of your land in its season and to
bless all the work of your hands.

∾ Deuteronomy 28:12 RSV ∿

Trouble is a steppingstone

Trouble is something no one can escape –
Everyone has it in some form or shape.
Some people hide it way down deep inside,
Some people bear it with gallant-like pride.
Some people worry and complain of their lot,
Some people covet what they haven't got
While others rebel and become bitter and old
With hopes that are dead and hearts that are
cold.
But the wise man accepts whatever God sends,
Willing to yield like a storm-tossed tree bends,
Knowing that God never made a mistake,
So whatever He sends they are willing to
take.
For trouble is part and parcel of life,
And no man can grow without struggle or
strife,
The steep hills ahead and the high mountain
peaks
Afford man at last the peace that he seeks ...
So blessed are the people who learn to accept
The trouble men try to escape and reject,
For in our acceptance we're given great grace

And courage and faith and the strength to face
The daily troubles that come to us all,
So we may learn to stand straight and tall ...
For the grandeur of life is born of defeat,
And in overcoming we make life complete.

We work hard with our own hands.
When we are cursed, we bless; when
we are persecuted, we endure it; when
we are slandered, we answer kindly.

❦ 1 Corinthians 4:12-13 NIV ❧

Priceless treasures

What could I give you that would truly please
In topsy-turvy times like these?
I can't take away or even make less
The things that annoy, disturb, and distress,
For stores don't sell a single thing
To make the heart that's troubled sing.
They sell rare gifts that are ultra-smart
But nothing to warm or comfort the heart.
The joys of life that cheer and bless
The stores don't sell, I must confess,
But friends and prayers are priceless treasures
Beyond all monetary measures,
And so I say a special prayer
That God will keep you in His care,
And if I can ever help you, dear,
In any way throughout the year,
You've only to call, for as long as I live,
Such as I have I freely give.

> *I bless the Lord who gives me counsel;*
> *in the night also my heart instructs me.*

> ❧ Psalm 16:7 RSV ☙

Blessings come in many guises

❧ ❧

When troubles come and things go wrong
And days are cheerless and nights are long,
We find it so easy to give in to despair
By magnifying the burdens we bear.
We add to our worries by refusing to try
To look for the rainbow in an overcast sky,
And the blessings God sent in a darkened disguise
Our troubled hearts failed to recognize,
Not knowing God sent it not to distress us
But to strengthen our faith and redeem and bless us.

Blessed is the man you discipline, O Lord:
the man you teach from your law.

❧ Psalm 94:12 NIV ❧

Blessing of
God's seasons

❧   ❧

We know we must pass
    through the seasons God sends,
Content in the knowledge
    that everything ends,
And, oh, what a blessing
    to know there are reasons
And to find that our souls
    must, too, have their seasons –
Bounteous seasons and barren ones, too,
    times for rejoicing and times to be blue –
But meeting these seasons of dark desolation
    with the strength that is born of anticipation
Comes from knowing that every season of sadness
    will surely be followed by a springtime of
gladness.

*Blessed is the man who walks not in the counsel
of the wicked, ... on his law he meditates day and
night. He is like a tree planted by streams of water,
that yields its fruit in its season, and its leaf does
not wither. In all that he does, he prospers.*

❧ Psalm 1:1-3 RSV ❧

It takes the bitter and sweet

∂∂ ∂∂

Life is a mixture
    of sunshine and rain,
Laughter and teardrops,
    pleasure and pain,
Low tides and high tides,
    mountains and plains,
Triumphs, defeats,
    and losses and gains,
But always in all ways
    or some dread affliction,
Be assured that it comes
    with God's kind benediction,
And if we accept it
    as a gift of His love,
We'll be showered with blessings
    from our Father above.

Taste and see that the Lord
is good; blessed is the man
who takes refuge in him.

∂∂ Psalm 34:8 NIV ∂∂

Take time
to appreciate
God's blessings

ɤ ɥ

Blessings are all around us.
If we look we can recognize a blessing in
each day, each hour, each minute,
each family member, each friend, each neighbor,
each community, each city, each nation,
each challenge, each word of encouragement,
each flower, each sunbeam, each raindrop,
each awesome wonder crafted by God,
each star, each sea, each bird, each tree,
each sorrow, each disappointment,
each faith, each prayer.

The list is endless and so are the blessings which
God has bestowed upon us. Train yourself to
recognize and appreciate the many blessings in
your life.

– Virginia J. Ruehlmann –

Blessed be your glorious name, and may it
be exalted above all blessing and praise. You
alone are the Lord. You made the heavens,
even the highest heavens, and all their starry
host, the earth and all that is on it, the seas and
all that is in them. You give life to everything,
and the multitudes of heaven worship you.

❧ Nehemiah 9:5-6 NIV ☙

Thanks for the blessings

When I count my blessings,
  I count my fans as one,
For without fans and friends,
  the writing I have done
Would lose all its meaning,
  its warmth, and its sincereness,
For how could I write
  without feeling a nearness
To all the dear people
  who interpret each line
With their own love and kindness,
  which become part of mine.
So, more than you know,
  I thank God up above
For fans, friends, and family
  and their gifts of love.

– *Helen Steiner Rice* –

*The blessing of the Lord makes rich,
and he adds no sorrow with it.*

Proverbs 10:22 RSV